An AMBUSH of TIGERS

A Wild Gathering of Collective Nouns

Betsy R. Rosenthal

Illustrated by Jago

M Millbrook Press/Minneapolis

For my family of humans—Dave, Adam, Sara, and Joel—and my group of writers, Ann and Sonya —B.R.R.

For my lovely family—Alex, Lily, and Rudy —Jago

Millbrook Press
A division of Lerner Publishing Group, Inc.
241 First Avenue North
Minneapolis, MN 55401 USA.

For reading levels and more information, look up this title at www.lernerbooks.com.

Main body text set in Blockhead Unplugged 20/23.
Typeface provided by Emigre.

Library of Congress Cataloging-in-Publication Data

Rosenthal, Betsy R.
   An ambush of tigers : A wild gathering of collective nouns / By Betsy R. Rosenthal ; Illustrated by Jago.
      pages   cm.
   ISBN 978-1-4677-1464-8 (lib. bdg. : alk. paper)
   ISBN 978-1-4677-6298-4 (EB)
   1. English language — Collective nouns — Juvenile literature. 2. English language — Rhymes — Juvenile literature. 3. English language — Grammar — Juvenile literature. I. Jago, illustrator. II. Title.
PE1689.R66 2015
372.61 — dc23   2014009383

Manufactured in the United States of America
1 – DP – 12/31/14

Do you ever wonder
what animals do
when they gather in groups
of more than two?

Does a tower of giraffes
way up high
spy a raft of otters
floating by?

Do leaps of leopards
jump into trees
while armies of herring
march in the seas?

Does a pack of wolves
load up bags for vacation?

Does a cast of hawks get a standing ovation?

Should a crash of rhinos
stay off the street
and a shiver of sharks
turn up the heat?

Does a team of oxen
lose every race?
A bouquet of pheasants
fit in a vase?

Would a labor of moles
wear polka-dot ties
when it goes to work
for a business of flies?

Who cleans up
when a clutter of cats
gets fooled by the pranks
of a mischief of rats?

Does a prickle of porcupines
feel any pain?
Can a flush of mallards
get sucked down the drain?

When a murder of crows leaves barely a trace, is a sleuth of bears hot on the case?

Should a stand of flamingos
be offered a seat
by a host of sparrows
who invite them to eat?

Can a parcel of penguins
be sent in the mail?
An intrusion of roaches
be thrown into jail?

Does a string of ponies
that's knotted and tied
stop a drove of sheep
to ask for a ride?

Would you buy cookies
from a troop of kangaroos
who use their pouches
for collecting the dues?

Should a walk of snails
get out of the way
of a rumba of rattlesnakes
dancing all day?

Does an ambush of tigers
quietly creep
past a bed of oysters
that snores in its sleep?

When a band of gorillas
sets up to play,
does a stench of skunks
scare them away?

Does a lounge of lizards
bask in the sun
while a party of jays
is out looking for fun?

And when all these animals
receive an invitation
to come together
for a huge celebration,

would you call it a mob?
A sea? A crowd?
Whatever it is,
it sure is LOUD!

Glossary

What else do these names for animal groups mean? You probably already know most of them. Can you guess why each word is used for a certain animal?

ambush (tigers): an attack from a hiding place

army (herring): a large group of people trained to fight

band (gorillas): 1. a group of people who play music together. 2. to join together in a group to achieve something

bed (oysters): 1. a piece of furniture that you sleep on. 2. a place in a garden where flowers are planted. 3. the bottom of a body of water, as in "an ocean bed"

bouquet (pheasants): a bunch of picked or cut flowers

business (flies): a company that makes or sells things or provides a service

cast (hawks): the actors in a play, movie, or television program

clutter (cats): a mess made by filling up a place with stuff, such as papers or trinkets

crash (rhinos): 1. to collide with another vehicle or obstacle. 2. a sudden loud noise as of something breaking or hitting another object

drove (sheep): 1. past tense of drive. 2. a large herd of animals being moved as a group, as in "The shepherd moved a drove of cattle to greener pastures."

flush (mallards): to flood something with water as a way of cleaning it

host (sparrows): a person who entertains guests

intrusion (roaches): forcing your way into a place or situation where you are not wanted or invited

labor (moles): to work hard

leap (leopards): jump or spring a long way, to a great height, or with great force

lounge (lizards): 1. to stand, sit, or lie in a lazy or relaxed way. 2. a comfortable room where people can sit and relax

mischief (rats): playful behavior that may annoy or harm others murder (crows): to kill someone deliberately (not by accident)

pack (wolves): 1. to put clothes or objects into a container (for example, a suitcase, box, or bag) to carry to another place or to store. 2. a group or package of related objects, such as a pack of cards

parcel (penguins): a package, or something that is packed, wrapped, or put into a box

party (jays): 1. an organized event where people enjoy themselves in a group. 2. a group of people working together

prickle (porcupines): a small, sharp point, such as a thorn; or what you feel if you touch one

raft (otters): a floating platform often made from logs tied together

rumba (rattlesnakes): a rhythmic dance that comes from Cuba and involves lots of hip movement

shiver (sharks): to shake with cold or fear

sleuth (bears): a detective, or anyone good at finding information

stand (flamingos): 1. to be on your feet with your body upright, or to get up from sitting. 2. an object on which you put things, as in a music stand

stench (skunks): a strong, unpleasant smell

string (ponies): 1. a thin cord or rope. 2. to put a row of objects on a piece of string or wire

team (oxen): a group of people who work together or play a sport together

tower (giraffes): a tall structure that is thin in relation to its height

troop (kangaroos): an organized group of soldiers, scouts, etc.

walk (snails): 1. to travel on foot. 2. a journey on foot